I0410249

FINANCIAL FREEDOM MADE SIMPLE

A Step-by-Step Guide to Wealth Creation and Money Management

Patrick Odega

Copyright © 2023 Patrick Odega

All rights reserved.

ISBN:

Dedication:

To all those who have dreamt of a life unburdened by financial stress,

and to those who strive to turn those dreams into a reality.

May this book serve as a guiding light on your journey to financial freedom,

offering clarity, wisdom, and practical steps towards wealth creation and money management.

With unwavering dedication and heartfelt gratitude,

this book is dedicated to you.

Table of Contents

Conclusion

Introduction:

Welcome to "Financial Freedom Made Simple: A Step-by-Step Guide to Wealth Creation and Money Management." This book is your key to unlocking the door to a life of financial independence and security. Whether you're just starting your journey towards financial freedom or seeking to strengthen your existing financial foundation, this comprehensive guide will provide you with the tools, knowledge, and strategies to navigate the path with confidence.

Chapter 1: Assessing Your Current Financial Situation will set the stage for your financial transformation. By gaining a clear understanding of your net worth, income, expenses, and debt, you will be able to identify areas that require attention and improvement. Armed with this knowledge, you'll be better prepared to create a solid financial plan tailored to your unique circumstances.

Chapter 2: Setting Financial Goals is the crucial next step. We will explore the art of defining clear and actionable financial goals, both in the short-term and long-term. By creating SMART goals Specific, Measurable, Achievable, Relevant, and Time-bound you'll be equipped to stay focused and motivated throughout your financial journey.

In Chapter 3: Building an Emergency Fund, we emphasize the importance of having a financial safety net. Unforeseen circumstances can arise at any time, and having an emergency fund in place provides the peace of mind and financial security necessary to weather life's unexpected storms.

Chapter 4: Creating a Solid Savings Plan will show you how to establish and maintain a disciplined savings strategy. Whether you're saving for a specific goal or building a buffer for future opportunities, the right savings plan will accelerate your path to financial freedom.

Chapter 5: Diving into Investing will demystify the world of investments and demonstrate how to make your money work for you. From stocks and bonds to real estate and other investment options, you'll learn how to build a diversified portfolio suited to your risk tolerance and financial objectives.

Chapter 6: Retirement Planning is a critical aspect of securing your financial future. We'll delve into the importance of early retirement planning, exploring various retirement accounts and strategies to ensure a comfortable and worry-free retirement.

In Chapter 7: Managing Debt Effectively, we tackle the burden of debt head-on. By implementing effective debt management strategies, you can regain control of your finances and pave the way for wealth accumulation.

Chapter 8: Smart Tax Planning unveils the power of strategic tax planning in wealth creation. Discover legitimate ways to minimize tax liabilities and maximize your savings through tax-advantaged investment options.

Chapter 9: Building Multiple Streams of Income introduces you to the concept of diversifying your income sources. Explore the world of passive income, side hustles, and entrepreneurial ventures to expand your earning potential.

Chapter 10: Protecting Your Wealth emphasizes the need for insurance coverage and estate planning to safeguard your hard-earned wealth. By understanding these essential elements, you can ensure a lasting legacy for your loved ones.

Chapter 11: Navigating Economic Challenges equips you with the knowledge and mindset to overcome economic fluctuations. With the right strategies in place, you'll remain resilient and stay on track towards financial freedom despite economic uncertainties.

In the Conclusion, we will summarize the transformative journey you've undertaken and reiterate the fundamental principles that will lead you to success. Remember, this book is not just about reading; it's about taking action. The knowledge and guidance within these pages are your stepping stones to a life of financial freedom and abundance.

Now, let's embark on this journey together, and let "Financial Freedom Made Simple" be your trusted companion as you create a secure and prosperous future for yourself and your loved ones.

Chapter 1:

Assessing Your Current Financial Situation

Financial freedom begins with a clear understanding of your current financial situation. Assessing where you stand financially is the foundation upon which you'll build your path to wealth and security. In this chapter, we will introduce you to the concept of financial assessment, its importance, and how it empowers you to take control of your financial future.

Understanding Net Worth and How to Calculate It:

Your net worth is a vital metric that reveals your financial health at a glance. We'll dive deep into the definition of net worth, which is the difference between your total assets and liabilities. By learning how to calculate your net worth, you'll gain valuable insights into your wealth accumulation or potential debt burdens.

Identifying Assets and Liabilities:

Assets and liabilities form the core components of your net worth. In this section, we'll explore different types of assets, including cash, investments, real estate, and valuable possessions. Simultaneously, we'll examine various liabilities, such as mortgages, student loans, credit card debt, and other outstanding loans. Understanding your assets and liabilities is the first step to making informed financial decisions.

Evaluating Income and Expenses:

Knowing your income and expenses is fundamental to effective financial planning. We'll guide you through the process of evaluating your various sources of income, such as salary, bonuses, investment returns, and passive income. Additionally, we'll help you categorize and analyze your expenses, enabling you to identify areas for potential improvement and saving.

Creating a Budget and Tracking Spending Habits:

A well-crafted budget is a powerful tool to manage your finances efficiently. In this section, we'll show you how to create a realistic budget that aligns with your financial goals. We'll also introduce methods to track your spending habits, empowering you to stay on track and avoid overspending.

Analyzing Debt and Credit Score:

Debt can significantly impact your financial well-being. We'll guide you through a comprehensive analysis of your debts, helping you understand the different types of debt and their implications on your financial journey. Additionally, we'll explore the significance of your credit score, the factors influencing it, and its role in financial transactions.

Strategies to Reduce Debt and Build a Healthy Credit Score:

Tackling debt and improving your credit score are critical steps towards financial freedom. In this section, we'll provide you with actionable strategies to reduce debt effectively, such as the debt snowball and debt avalanche methods. You'll also learn how to build a healthy credit score through responsible credit management and timely payments.

 Having laid the groundwork for your journey to financial freedom through a thorough assessment of your current financial situation. Understanding your net worth, identifying assets and liabilities, evaluating income and expenses, creating a budget, and analyzing debt and credit score are critical steps that will shape your financial decisions and strategies moving forward.

However, the process of achieving financial freedom doesn't end with the assessment. Instead, it marks the beginning of a transformative journey towards building a secure and prosperous future. Armed with the insights gained in this chapter, let's explore some essential strategies to take control of your finances, reduce debt, and improve your credit score.

Strategies to Reduce Debt and Build a Healthy Credit Score

Creating a Debt Repayment Plan:

- Develop a personalized debt repayment plan tailored to your financial situation and priorities.
- Identify the most effective method to pay off debts, whether through the snowball approach (paying off smaller debts first) or the avalanche approach (tackling higher interest debts first).
- Establish a budget allocation dedicated to debt repayment and adhere to it consistently.

Negotiating with Creditors:

- Learn effective negotiation tactics to work with creditors and potentially reduce interest rates or negotiate more manageable repayment terms.
- Explore debt consolidation options that may simplify your payments and lower interest rates.

Building a Positive Credit History:

- Understand the factors influencing your credit score, such as payment history, credit utilization, length of credit history, new credit inquiries, and credit mix.
- Make timely payments and aim to maintain a low credit utilization ratio to positively impact your credit score.

Monitoring Your Credit Report:

- Regularly review your credit report to check for errors or inaccuracies that could negatively affect your credit score.
- Address any discrepancies promptly to ensure an accurate representation of your credit history.

Building a Healthy Credit Mix:

- Diversify your credit portfolio by maintaining a healthy mix of different credit types, such as credit cards, installment loans, and lines of credit.
- Avoid opening multiple new credit accounts simultaneously, as it may negatively impact your credit score.

By completing the financial assessment outlined in this chapter and implementing the strategies to reduce debt and build a healthy credit score, you have taken significant strides towards achieving financial freedom. Remember that financial freedom is a journey, and it requires commitment, discipline, and continuous improvement.

As we move forward in this guide, each subsequent chapter will build upon the foundation laid in Chapter 1. From setting financial goals and building an emergency fund to exploring investment opportunities and retirement planning, every step brings you closer to the life of financial abundance and security you envision.

Stay focused, remain resilient in the face of challenges, and celebrate your progress along the way. With determination and the principles outlined in this guide, you have the potential to turn your dreams into reality and embark on a lifelong journey towards financial freedom.

Chapter 2:

Setting Financial Goals

Financial freedom is not an arbitrary destination but a deliberate journey guided by well-defined financial goals. In this chapter, we will explore the significance of setting financial goals and how they serve as a roadmap for your financial success. By establishing clear objectives, you'll gain clarity, motivation, and direction in managing your finances and making sound financial decisions.

The Importance of Setting Financial Goals:

- Understand why setting financial goals is vital in achieving long-term financial security and fulfillment.
- Explore how financial goals provide focus, purpose, and a sense of accomplishment throughout your financial journey.

Defining Short-Term and Long-Term Goals:

- Distinguish between short-term and long-term financial goals, each playing a unique role in shaping your financial path.
- Discover the advantages of setting short-term goals to celebrate milestones and maintain momentum on your journey.

The SMART Goal-Setting Framework:

- Introduce the SMART framework: Specific, Measurable, Achievable, Relevant, and Time-bound.
- Learn how to apply the SMART criteria to your financial goals, making them more concrete and actionable.

Aligning Financial Goals with Personal Values and Aspirations:

- Recognize the importance of aligning your financial goals with your personal values and life aspirations.
- Understand how goal alignment enhances motivation and ensures that your financial journey remains purpose-driven.

Prioritizing Goals and Creating an Action Plan:

- Prioritize your financial goals based on urgency, importance, and achievability.
- Develop a step-by-step action plan for each goal, breaking them into manageable tasks with clear timelines.

Understanding the Difference Between Needs and Wants:

- Distinguish between needs and wants to ensure that your financial goals prioritize essential necessities.
- Avoid falling into the trap of overspending on discretionary items that may hinder your progress toward more significant financial milestones.

Setting Realistic and Attainable Goals:

- Assess your current financial situation to set goals that are challenging yet attainable.
- Avoid setting overly ambitious goals that could lead to frustration or financial strain.

Breaking Down Long-Term Goals into Short-Term Milestones:

- Convert long-term financial goals into smaller, manageable short-term milestones.
- Breaking down complex objectives makes them less daunting and allows you to celebrate achievements more frequently.

Measuring Progress and Tracking Success:

- Establish metrics to measure your progress toward each financial goal.
- Regularly review your achievements and make adjustments to your action plan if needed.

Creating Accountability and Seeking Support:

- Share your financial goals with a trusted friend, family member, or financial advisor to create a sense of accountability.
- Seek support from like-minded individuals or a financial community to stay motivated and exchange ideas.

The Power of Visualization and Affirmations:

- Utilize visualization techniques to see yourself accomplishing your financial goals.
- Use positive affirmations to reinforce your belief in your ability to achieve financial success.

Reassessing and Adjusting Goals:

- Life is dynamic, and circumstances may change. Be open to reassessing and adjusting your financial goals as needed.
- Adapt your action plan to accommodate unforeseen challenges or opportunities.

By setting clear, specific, and achievable financial goals, you have taken a significant step towards realizing your dreams of financial freedom. As you continue through this guide, remember that your goals are dynamic and may evolve over time. Stay focused on your vision, regularly review and track your progress, and be prepared to adapt your plan as circumstances change.

Each milestone you achieve brings you closer to the life of purpose, security, and prosperity you envision. Embrace the power of visualization and positive affirmations to strengthen your belief in your ability to achieve financial success. With determination and a well-structured action plan, you are well on your way to turning your financial aspirations into tangible achievements. The subsequent chapters will equip you with the tools and knowledge to further empower your financial journey, unlocking the doors to a future of abundance and fulfillment.

Chapter 3:

Building an Emergency Fund

Financial stability and preparedness are essential pillars of financial freedom. An emergency fund is a critical component of your financial safety net, providing you with the confidence and security to navigate unforeseen circumstances. In this chapter, we will explore the significance of building an emergency fund, determining its ideal size, where to keep it for easy access, and effective strategies to establish and maintain it.

Understanding the Significance of an Emergency Fund:

- Recognize the importance of an emergency fund as a buffer against unexpected financial challenges.
- Understand how an emergency fund safeguards your financial well-being during times of crisis, providing peace of mind and preventing the need to rely on high-interest debt.

Determining the Ideal Emergency Fund Size:

- Evaluate your unique financial situation to calculate the appropriate size for your emergency fund.
- Consider factors such as your monthly expenses, the stability of your income, and any potential risks or uncertainties.

Where to Keep Your Emergency Fund for Easy Access:

- Explore suitable options for storing your emergency fund, focusing on accessibility and safety.
- Consider keeping the funds in a separate savings account, money market account, or high-yield savings account that offers liquidity without penalty.

Strategies to Build and Maintain Your Emergency Fund:

- Establish a clear savings goal for your emergency fund and incorporate it into your budget.
- Automate your savings by setting up recurring transfers from your main

account to your emergency fund, ensuring consistent contributions.

- Use windfalls, such as tax refunds or bonuses, to bolster your emergency fund and expedite its growth.
- Redirect money saved from cutting unnecessary expenses into your emergency fund.
- Resist the temptation to dip into your emergency fund for non-emergencies by exercising discipline and self-control.
- Reevaluate and adjust your emergency fund size periodically to account for life changes, such as a new job, increased expenses, or changes in family dynamics.

Building an emergency fund is a critical step toward financial freedom and stability. As you work to establish this financial safety net, keep in mind that it is not a one-size-fits-all approach. The ideal size of your emergency fund depends on your individual circumstances, needs, and risk tolerance.

By understanding the significance of an emergency fund, determining its size, selecting an appropriate location for easy access, and implementing effective strategies to build and maintain it, you are taking proactive steps to secure your financial future. This chapter equips you with the knowledge and tools to protect yourself from unforeseen financial challenges, ensuring that you can stay on track toward achieving your broader financial goals.

As we progress through this guide, remember that an emergency fund is just one piece of the puzzle. In the subsequent chapters, we will continue to explore other essential aspects of financial freedom, including investing, retirement planning, debt management, and strategies to create multiple streams of income. Together, these components will form a comprehensive financial plan, empowering you to live a life of abundance and peace of mind.

Chapter 4:

Creating a Solid Savings Plan

Building a strong savings plan is a fundamental step towards achieving financial freedom. Savings serve as the building blocks of your financial foundation, providing security during tough times and opportunities to grow wealth. In this chapter, we will explore the importance of saving, different types of savings accounts and investment options, setting savings targets, automating savings, and effective strategies to maximize both savings and investment growth.

Importance of Saving for Financial Security and Opportunities:

Saving is more than just setting money aside; it's a powerful tool that offers financial security and opens doors to future opportunities. Whether it's for emergencies, major purchases, or long-term goals like retirement, having a robust savings plan is crucial for your overall financial well-being.

Types of Savings Accounts and Investment Options:

Understanding the various types of savings accounts and investment options available empowers you to make informed decisions that align with your financial goals and risk tolerance. Explore different savings accounts, money market accounts, certificates of deposit (CDs), and investment vehicles such as stocks, bonds, mutual funds, and real estate.

Setting Savings Targets Based on Financial Goals:

Identifying your financial goals and their associated costs allows you to set realistic savings targets. Whether you're saving for a down payment on a house, a dream vacation, or building an emergency fund, quantifying your objectives provides a clear roadmap for your savings plan.

Automating Savings for Consistency and Discipline:

Automating your savings is a powerful way to ensure consistency and discipline in your financial habits. Set up automatic transfers from your primary account to your savings or investment accounts on a regular basis. This way, your savings grow effortlessly, and you're less tempted to spend the money on impulsive purchases.

Strategies to Maximize Savings and Investment Growth:

Implementing strategies to maximize savings and investment growth accelerates your progress towards financial freedom. Consider the following strategies:

1. Budgeting and Expense Tracking: Create a budget to allocate funds for savings and track your expenses. Identifying areas where you can cut back on unnecessary spending allows you to redirect more money into savings and investments.

2. Pay Yourself First: Treat your savings as a priority expense by "paying yourself first" before spending on discretionary items. This practice ensures that you prioritize saving and investing in your financial plan.

3. Take Advantage of Employer Benefits: If your employer offers retirement plans

with matching contributions, take full advantage of this benefit. It's essentially free money that accelerates your retirement savings.

4. Dollar-Cost Averaging: For investments in the stock market, consider dollar-cost averaging, which involves investing a fixed amount at regular intervals. This approach reduces the impact of market fluctuations and may lead to better long-term results.

5. Reinvesting Dividends and Returns: When investing in dividend-paying stocks or funds, reinvest the dividends to compound your returns and grow your investments faster.

Creating a solid savings plan is the bedrock of your financial success. By recognizing the importance of saving, understanding various savings and investment options, setting savings targets, automating your savings, and implementing strategies to maximize growth, you are laying a strong foundation for financial freedom.

As you progress through this guide, each subsequent chapter will build upon the principles outlined in this chapter. From investing wisely and planning for retirement to managing debt and building multiple streams of income, your comprehensive financial plan will come together, empowering you to create the life you desire.

Stay committed to your financial goals, be disciplined in your savings habits, and be open to learning and adapting your strategies as needed. With dedication and informed decision-making, you are well on your way to achieving your dreams of financial freedom and a prosperous future.

Chapter 5:
Diving into Investing

Investing and Its Role in Wealth Creation:

Investing is a powerful tool for growing wealth and achieving long-term financial goals. In this chapter, we will explore the fundamentals of investing, its significance in wealth creation, and the key role it plays in your journey towards financial freedom. Understanding the principles of investing will empower you to make informed decisions and harness the potential of your money to work for you.

Different Investment Options:

There is a wide array of investment options available, each with its unique risk and return characteristics. We will delve into various investment vehicles, including:

1. Stocks: Ownership shares in publicly-traded companies, offering the potential for capital appreciation and dividends.

2. Bonds: Debt securities issued by governments or corporations, providing fixed interest payments over time.

3. Mutual Funds: Pooled investments that combine funds from multiple investors to invest in a diversified portfolio of stocks, bonds, or other assets.

4. Real Estate: Investing in properties for rental income or potential appreciation in value.

5. Exchange-Traded Funds (ETFs): Similar to mutual funds, but they trade on stock exchanges like individual stocks.

6. Retirement Accounts: Tax-advantaged accounts like 401(k)s and IRAs designed to facilitate long-term retirement savings.

Assessing Risk Tolerance and Investment Horizon:

Before diving into investments, it's essential to assess your risk tolerance and investment horizon. Your risk tolerance reflects your ability to handle fluctuations in the value of your investments, while your investment horizon defines the length of time you plan to hold your investments. By understanding these factors, you can tailor your investment strategy to align with your comfort level and financial goals.

Diversifying Investment Portfolio for Optimal Returns:

Diversification is a crucial risk management strategy that involves spreading your investments across different asset classes and industries. By diversifying your portfolio, you reduce the impact of individual investment performance on your overall wealth. We will explore the benefits of diversification and techniques for creating a well-balanced investment portfolio.

Monitoring and Adjusting Investment Strategies Over Time:

The financial markets are dynamic, and economic conditions change over time. Monitoring your investments regularly allows you to stay informed about their performance. We will discuss how to evaluate your investments, the importance of periodic reviews, and when to make adjustments to your investment strategies based on changing circumstances.

Investing is a key driver of wealth creation and long-term financial success. By understanding the different investment options available, assessing your risk tolerance and investment horizon, diversifying your portfolio, and monitoring and adjusting your investment strategies over time, you will be better equipped to make informed investment decisions that align with your financial goals.

As you progress through this guide, you will continue to build on your knowledge of investing, retirement planning, debt management, and other crucial aspects of financial freedom. Remember that investing is not a one-time event but an ongoing process that requires patience, discipline, and a long-term perspective. By following sound investment principles and staying committed to your financial goals, you can harness the power of investing to achieve the life of abundance and security you desire.

Chapter 6:

Retirement Planning

Retirement planning is a critical aspect of achieving financial freedom and ensuring a comfortable future. In this chapter, we will emphasize the importance of retirement planning, providing you with the tools and knowledge to navigate the various retirement accounts, calculate your retirement needs, set savings targets, and develop long-term financial strategies to secure a fulfilling retirement.

Understanding the Need for Retirement Planning:

Retirement planning is not a luxury but a necessity. We will discuss the importance of preparing for retirement early in your career to avoid potential financial challenges later in life. By understanding the impact of inflation, rising healthcare costs, and increased life expectancy, you'll recognize the significance of starting your retirement journey as soon as possible.

Exploring Retirement Accounts (401(k), IRA, Roth IRA, etc.):

Retirement accounts are valuable tools for tax-advantaged retirement savings. We will explore popular retirement account options such as 401(k)s, Traditional IRAs, Roth IRAs, and other employer-sponsored plans. Understanding the benefits, contribution limits, and tax implications of each account will allow you to make informed decisions about which accounts align best with your financial goals.

Calculating Retirement Needs and Setting Savings Targets:

Determining how much money you'll need for a comfortable retirement is essential. We will guide you through the process of calculating your retirement needs based on factors such as desired lifestyle, expected expenses, and estimated life expectancy. Armed with this knowledge, you can set savings targets to meet your retirement goals.

Strategies to Catch Up on Retirement Savings if Starting Late:

If you find yourself behind on retirement savings, don't despair. We will explore strategies to catch up on retirement savings, including maximizing contributions to retirement accounts, taking advantage of catch-up contributions, and considering more aggressive investment approaches to grow your savings faster.

Long-Term Financial Planning for a Comfortable Retirement:

Long-term financial planning involves developing a comprehensive strategy that encompasses all aspects of your retirement journey. We will discuss ways to manage potential risks, such as inflation, market fluctuations, and healthcare costs. Additionally, we will explore how to balance your investment portfolio to align with your retirement timeline and risk tolerance.

Retirement planning is a fundamental element of your financial journey and requires diligent consideration and action. By understanding the need for retirement planning, exploring various retirement accounts, calculating your retirement needs, and setting savings targets, you are taking significant steps towards securing a fulfilling and comfortable retirement.

Remember that retirement planning is not a one-time event; it requires continuous monitoring and adjustment as life circumstances change. By adopting proactive strategies to catch up on retirement savings if you're starting late and implementing long-term financial planning, you can create a solid foundation for a financially secure and enjoyable retirement.

As you progress through this guide, continue to build upon your retirement planning knowledge and integrate it with other financial aspects such as investing, debt management, and multiple income streams. By combining these elements, you can pave the way to financial freedom, allowing you to retire with confidence and embark on new adventures during your golden years.

Chapter 7:

Managing Debt Effectively

Debt can be a significant obstacle on your path to financial freedom. In this chapter, we will explore strategies to manage different types of debt, implement effective debt repayment methods such as the snowball and avalanche approaches, consider consolidation and refinancing options, and develop a debt-free mindset to avoid common debt traps.

Strategies to Tackle Different Types of Debt:

Different types of debt require distinct approaches. We will discuss strategies for managing various debts, including credit card debt, student loans, personal loans, and mortgages. By understanding the characteristics of each debt and developing targeted repayment plans, you can regain control of your financial well-being.

Snowball and Avalanche Methods for Debt Repayment:

Two popular methods for debt repayment are the snowball and avalanche methods. The snowball approach involves paying off the smallest debts first, providing a psychological boost and momentum as you eliminate individual debts. The avalanche method, on the other hand, focuses on paying off debts with the highest interest rates first, saving money on interest over time. We will compare these methods and help you choose the one that best suits your needs and preferences.

Consolidation and Refinancing Options:

Debt consolidation and refinancing can be useful tools to simplify your debt management and potentially reduce interest rates. We will explore options such as debt consolidation loans, balance transfer credit cards, and mortgage refinancing, discussing their advantages and potential pitfalls.

Avoiding Common Debt Traps and Maintaining a Debt-Free Mindset:

It's essential to be aware of common debt traps and avoid falling into them. We will discuss how to resist impulsive spending, manage credit card usage responsibly, and distinguish between needs and wants to maintain financial discipline. Cultivating a debt-free mindset and understanding the true cost of debt will empower you to make informed financial decisions.

Effectively managing debt is crucial for achieving financial freedom and securing a stable financial future. By implementing strategies to tackle different types of debt, choosing suitable debt repayment methods, exploring consolidation and refinancing options, and developing a debt-free mindset, you can take control of your financial situation and work towards a debt-free life.

As you progress through this guide, continue to apply these principles in conjunction with other financial strategies such as budgeting, saving, investing, and retirement planning. With perseverance, determination, and a commitment to responsible financial habits, you can break free from the burden of debt and pave the way to a life of financial security and abundance.

Chapter 8:
Smart Tax Planning

Tax planning is a crucial aspect of achieving financial freedom and optimizing wealth creation. In this chapter, we will explore the impact of taxes on your financial journey, legal ways to minimize tax liabilities, the benefits of tax-advantaged investment accounts, tax-efficient strategies for retirement planning, and the importance of consulting with tax professionals to receive personalized advice.

Understanding the Impact of Taxes on Wealth Creation:

Taxes can significantly impact your ability to accumulate and grow wealth. By understanding various tax implications, including income tax, capital gains tax, and estate tax, you can make informed financial decisions that optimize your after-tax returns and accelerate your progress towards financial freedom.

Legal Ways to Minimize Tax Liabilities:

There are numerous legal strategies to minimize tax liabilities. From maximizing deductions and tax credits to structuring your investments and income in a tax-efficient manner, we will explore practical ways to reduce your tax burden while remaining compliant with tax laws.

Utilizing Tax-Advantaged Investment Accounts:

Tax-advantaged investment accounts offer unique benefits and incentives that can boost your wealth-building efforts. We will discuss popular tax-advantaged accounts such as Individual Retirement Accounts (IRAs), Roth IRAs, 401(k)s, and Health Savings Accounts (HSAs), highlighting their respective advantages and eligibility criteria.

Tax-Efficient Strategies for Retirement Planning:

Retirement planning involves considering the tax implications of your savings and investment decisions. By utilizing tax-efficient strategies, such as balancing contributions to traditional and Roth retirement accounts, you can optimize your retirement income and potentially reduce tax liabilities during your retirement years.

Consulting with Tax Professionals for Personalized Advice:

While this chapter provides valuable insights into smart tax planning, it's essential to recognize that everyone's financial situation is unique. Consulting with tax professionals, such as certified public accountants (CPAs) or tax advisors, can provide personalized advice tailored to your specific circumstances. A tax professional can help you navigate complex tax laws, identify opportunities for tax savings, and ensure compliance with tax regulations.

Smart tax planning is a crucial component of your overall financial strategy, enabling you to maximize your wealth creation and safeguard your financial future. By understanding the impact of taxes on wealth accumulation, employing legal methods to minimize tax liabilities, utilizing tax-advantaged investment accounts, implementing tax-efficient retirement planning strategies, and seeking guidance from tax professionals, you can make informed decisions that optimize your after-tax income and accelerate your journey to financial freedom.

As you progress through this guide, continue to integrate smart tax planning with other financial aspects such as budgeting, investing, and debt management. Each element plays a critical role in building a comprehensive financial plan that aligns with your goals and aspirations. By taking a proactive approach to tax planning and staying informed about tax laws and changes, you can position yourself for financial success and confidently navigate the complexities of the tax landscape.

Chapter 9:

Building Multiple Streams of Income

Building multiple streams of income is a powerful strategy that can significantly impact your path to financial freedom. In this chapter, we will explore the importance of diversifying income sources, the potential of passive income opportunities such as rental properties and dividends, the value of side hustles and entrepreneurial ventures, and how to strike a balance between managing multiple income streams while ensuring a healthy work-life integration. By embracing the concept of diversification, you can create resilience in your financial journey and open up new possibilities for wealth creation.

The Power of Diversifying Income Sources:

Relying solely on a single source of income can be risky, as economic fluctuations and unforeseen events can impact your financial stability. Diversifying income sources spreads your risk and provides a safety net during challenging times. We will explore the benefits of having multiple streams of income and how it can improve your financial security.

Exploring Passive Income Opportunities:

Passive income is money earned with minimal ongoing effort or active involvement. We will discuss various passive income opportunities, such as rental properties, dividend-paying stocks, peer-to-peer lending, and digital assets like e-books or online courses. By generating passive income streams, you can build wealth while having more flexibility with your time.

Side Hustles and Entrepreneurial Ventures:

Side hustles and entrepreneurial ventures offer opportunities to turn your skills, hobbies, or passions into profitable ventures. We will explore different side hustle ideas and discuss how to start and grow your own business. Embracing entrepreneurship can not only create additional income streams but also foster personal growth and fulfillment.

Balancing Time and Effort for Multiple Income Streams:

Managing multiple income streams requires effective time management and prioritization. We will discuss strategies for balancing your time and effort across various income-generating activities, ensuring that each stream receives the attention it deserves while avoiding burnout.

Building Resilience through Diversified Income Sources:

By building multiple streams of income, you create a more resilient financial foundation. This resilience can shield you from the negative impacts of a job loss, economic downturns, or changes in industry trends. We will explore how diversification can act as a buffer against unforeseen circumstances and provide peace of mind during challenging times.

Building multiple streams of income is a transformative approach that can revolutionize your financial life. By embracing diversification, exploring passive income opportunities, venturing into side hustles and entrepreneurship, and balancing your time and effort effectively, you can create a more secure and prosperous future. The power of multiple income streams lies not only in their ability to generate wealth but also in the sense of empowerment and fulfillment they bring.

As you progress through this guide, continue to explore and implement strategies for diversifying your income. Embrace the opportunities that align with your skills, interests, and financial goals. By developing multiple streams of income, you can achieve greater financial independence, flexibility, and peace of mind, ultimately moving closer to the life of abundance and freedom you desire.

Chapter 10:

Protecting Your Wealth

As you work towards financial freedom and wealth creation, it's essential to protect the assets and resources you've accumulated. In this chapter, we will explore the significance of insurance coverage for financial protection, the various types of insurance to consider, the importance of estate planning and wealth transfer strategies, and how to create a comprehensive safety net to safeguard your family and assets.

Importance of Insurance Coverage for Financial Protection:

Insurance serves as a critical tool in mitigating financial risks and providing protection for you and your loved ones. We will discuss the importance of insurance coverage in safeguarding against unexpected events, such as medical emergencies, accidents, natural disasters, and unforeseen liabilities.

Types of Insurance to Consider:

Various types of insurance exist to cater to different aspects of your life. We will explore the most common ones, including:

1. **Life Insurance:** Provides a financial safety net for your loved ones in the event of your passing, offering them financial security and support.

2. **Health Insurance:** Helps cover medical expenses, protecting you from the high costs of healthcare.

3. **Home Insurance:** Protects your property against damages or losses due to fire, theft, or other covered perils.

4. Auto Insurance: Offers coverage for your vehicles, including liability protection and coverage for damages.

5. **Disability Insurance:** Provides income replacement if you are unable to work due to a disability.

6. **Liability Insurance:** Protects you from legal liabilities in case of accidents or injuries

that occur on your property or as a result of your actions.

Estate Planning and Wealth Transfer Strategies:

Estate planning involves creating a comprehensive plan to manage your assets and ensure their smooth transfer to your beneficiaries after your passing. We will discuss the importance of having a will, trusts, and other legal documents to avoid complications and protect your family's financial well-being.

Creating a Comprehensive Safety Net for Your Family and Assets:

By combining insurance coverage, estate planning, and other protective measures, you can create a comprehensive safety net for your family and assets. This safety net will provide financial security and peace of mind during challenging times, ensuring that your loved ones are well taken care of and your hard-earned wealth is preserved.

Protecting your wealth is an integral part of your financial journey. By recognizing the importance of insurance coverage, exploring different types of insurance to consider, implementing estate planning and wealth transfer strategies, and creating a comprehensive safety net, you are taking proactive steps to safeguard your family and assets.

As you progress through this guide, continue to prioritize protection alongside wealth creation. By incorporating insurance coverage and estate planning into your financial plan, you are building a solid foundation for long-term financial security. With each measure you put in place, you create greater resilience and stability, empowering you to pursue your financial goals with confidence and peace of mind.

Chapter 11:

Navigating Economic Challenges

Economic cycles are an inevitable part of the financial landscape, with periods of growth, recession, and recovery affecting individuals and businesses alike. In this chapter, we will explore the significance of understanding economic cycles and their impact on personal finance. We will also discuss strategies to safeguard your finances during economic downturns, the role of diversification and long-term perspective, and the importance of seeking opportunities amidst economic challenges.

Understanding Economic Cycles and Their Impact on Personal Finance:

Economic cycles, characterized by expansions and contractions, have a significant impact on personal finance. During economic expansions, opportunities for growth and prosperity arise, but periods of recession can bring financial challenges. By understanding these cycles and their potential effects on income, investments, and job stability, you can proactively prepare for economic fluctuations.

Strategies to Safeguard Finances During Economic Downturns:

During economic downturns, it's crucial to take measures to safeguard your finances. We will explore strategies such as:

1. Emergency Fund: Having an adequate emergency fund provides a financial cushion during unexpected job loss or income reduction.

2. Debt Management: Reducing debt during economic expansions can lighten the burden during downturns.

3. Budgeting: Creating and sticking to a budget helps manage expenses and preserve financial stability.

4. Reviewing Investments: Reevaluating your investment portfolio and adjusting it based on risk tolerance and economic conditions can protect your wealth.

The Role of Diversification and Long-Term Perspective:

Diversification is a powerful risk management strategy during economic challenges. By spreading investments across different asset classes, industries, and geographical regions, you can reduce the impact of market volatility on your portfolio. Additionally, maintaining a long-term perspective allows you to ride out short-term market fluctuations and benefit from the potential growth of your investments over time.

Seeking Opportunities Amidst Economic Challenges:

Economic challenges can present unique opportunities for growth and investment. We will discuss how to identify undervalued assets, consider alternative investments, and capitalize on potential market upswings. By remaining vigilant and adaptable, you can seize opportunities that may arise during economic downturns.

Navigating economic challenges is an essential skill in achieving financial freedom. By understanding economic cycles and their impact on personal finance, implementing strategies to safeguard your finances during downturns, embracing diversification and a long-term perspective, and seeking opportunities amidst challenges, you can navigate economic fluctuations with confidence.

As you progress through this guide, continue to stay informed about economic conditions and their potential effects on your financial situation. By incorporating the strategies outlined in this chapter, you can build resilience in the face of economic uncertainties and position yourself to thrive in both prosperous and challenging times. Remember that financial freedom is not merely about avoiding obstacles but also about leveraging opportunities to achieve your goals and create a prosperous future.

Conclusion:

Throughout this guide, we have embarked on a transformative journey towards financial freedom and a financially secure future. We explored essential principles and strategies that can empower you to take control of your finances and shape the life you desire. Let's recapitulate the key aspects of this journey and offer encouragement and motivation to take decisive action towards your financial goals.

Recapitulating the Journey to Financial Freedom:

1. Assessing Your Current Financial Situation: We began by understanding our current financial standing, calculating net worth, evaluating income and expenses, and creating a budget. This foundation provided clarity on where we stand and where we aim to go.

2. Setting Financial Goals: We recognized the importance of setting clear and achievable financial goals. By defining short-term and long-term objectives and using the SMART

goal-setting framework, we outlined a roadmap for our financial success.

3. Building an Emergency Fund: Creating an emergency fund became a priority to handle unforeseen circumstances and provide a safety net during challenging times.

4. Creating a Solid Savings Plan: With a savings plan in place, we explored various savings accounts, investment options, and strategies to maximize growth, ensuring we have resources to pursue our dreams.

5. Diving into Investing: Understanding investing allowed us to harness the power of compound growth and diversification, further accelerating our path to financial freedom.

6. Managing Debt Effectively: By tackling different types of debt and implementing smart debt repayment methods, we liberated ourselves from financial burdens and achieved greater financial flexibility.

7. Retirement Planning: Retirement planning provided us with a clear vision of our golden years, enabling us to set savings targets and

take advantage of tax-advantaged retirement accounts.

8. Building Multiple Streams of Income: We embraced diversification and explored passive income opportunities, side hustles, and entrepreneurial ventures to create resilience and unlock new wealth-building possibilities.

9. Protecting Your Wealth: Safeguarding our assets and securing our family's future through insurance coverage, estate planning, and a comprehensive safety net became a vital component of our financial strategy.

10. Navigating Economic Challenges: Understanding economic cycles and implementing strategies during economic downturns fortified our financial foundation, allowing us to capitalize on opportunities and remain steadfast in our pursuit of financial freedom.

Encouragement and Motivation for Readers to Take Action:

As we conclude this journey, I want to encourage you to take action and implement the valuable insights you've gained. The path to financial freedom may have its challenges, but every step forward counts. Remember that progress is not about achieving perfection but about consistently moving in the right direction. Celebrate your successes, learn from your setbacks, and stay committed to your financial goals.

Parting Words of Wisdom for a Financially Secure Future:

Financial freedom is not just about amassing wealth but also about creating a life of purpose, fulfillment, and security. Embrace financial education as a lifelong pursuit, continually seeking knowledge and adapting your strategies to align with your evolving circumstances and aspirations.

Be mindful of your spending habits, invest wisely, and prioritize saving for the future. Take care of your physical and mental well-being, as they contribute to your financial success. Surround yourself with a supportive community of like-minded individuals who share your financial goals, as collective encouragement and accountability can propel you towards success.

In times of doubt or uncertainty, remember that small steps, consistently taken, lead to significant progress. And most importantly, stay true to your values and dreams. Financial freedom is not a destination; it's a journey of self-discovery, growth, and empowerment.

As you move forward, embrace the challenges and opportunities that come your way. Believe in your ability to create the life you envision and commit to taking control of your financial destiny. You have the power to shape your financial future, and with perseverance, determination, and resilience, you can achieve the life of abundance and freedom you deserve.

www.ingramcontent.com/pod-product-compliance
Lightning Source LLC
Chambersburg PA
CBHW062251290526
45794CB00006B/2502